primmychorley

Black Dollies

contents

Goodbye Lavender,
changes are coming and
we must leave you young and
ALKANET and VIOLET, crystal in
the abbey to the wall you
and our secret walk
stopping jack
Goodbye Babs and Nora
Don and Nora
Palaki's shop, Station Rd
Church Street
Goodbye...

Goodbye my friend Dorothy...
...picked those huge black
berries on a little table
on the front door
I shall be ringing
never knowing
you are soon to die.
Goodbye to the
Abbey bell. We
hear you ringing
right across
the fields to
Mole End at spring
-ett's HILL
I'm Jack

Textile artist Primmy Chorley brings together the vernacular and family memories to create pieces full of movement, colour and figures of lively activity. Originally training in the classic, traditional technical practices of drawing, she ultimately abandoned that for embroidery – which she felt enabled her to work in a way that better reflected how she actually saw the world. Although linked to a strong tradition of vernacular or folk art practice and history, Primmy Chorley is currently taking this in a unique direction.

Primmy's embroidery is about things that have occurred in her life – showing herself, family and pets in a diary of memory – sad things often feature, as the stitching can act as a refuge or counter-balance to unpleasant times. Her pieces are mostly wool on wool backgrounds, and include appliqué and stitched writing – often with additional fragments or lengths stitched onto the main piece (reflecting the making process of quilting, which is also a strong interest). Primmy keeps sketchbooks of ideas – mainly writing and poems, song lyrics or something heard on the radio. Also drawings to remember things seen for future use in her embroideries – old china in a museum, old clothes, or the detail of a carving on an ancient building. These gradually form the idea for a complete piece that she will see in her head. However, no piece is planned before being started, instead they grow organically into a particular theme or picture that she has imagined. It is this flexibility that means she does not use a frame or stretcher, since this enables her to take work in progress with her wherever she goes, incorporating chance developments or surprises along the way.

During the process of researching a solo exhibition one inevitably talks to a great number of people about the artist and their work. I would like to thank all those who helped in the exhibition and in the production of this publication. We are most grateful to everyone who has worked so hard to make this exhibition happen, in particular Audrey Walker, Christine Mills, Eleri Mills, Rozanne Hawksley and Eirian and Denys Short all of whom were unequivocal in their assessment of Primmy's importance and uniqueness. I am particularly grateful to Dr Jennifer Harris, Deputy Director and Curator of Textiles at the Whitworth Art Gallery in Manchester, author of several influential publications on textiles including *Five Thousand Years of Textiles* and curator of several major exhibitions including *The Subversive Stitch* in 1988, who visited Primmy Chorley and wrote the following essay.

This is Primmy's first solo exhibition and presents a unique opportunity to see a range of pieces from this important textile artist – so finally thanks to Primmy for allowing us to view part of her private world of stitch. The exhibition will be shown at The Gallery, Ruthin Craft Centre during spring 2001.

Philip Hughes
Gallery Director
Ruthin Craft Centre

left: Goodbye Lavenders Road – *right:* Mrs Tibby

Lavenders Road

A Marriage

On the 12th day of February Jessie We lived at Mole End cottage at Springetts Hill WEST MALLING in KENT.

f you ask to be shown her work Primmy Chorley suggests that you pay her a visit in her tiny stone-built cottage on a hillside in Gwynedd, North Wales where her highly distinctive figurative embroideries form what she describes as the 'wallpaper' – pinned to the walls, unframed, in a higgledy-piggledy manner, decorating clothing made for her (now grown-up) children, made up into tea cosies or oddly expressionless, but somehow compelling angel 'dolls' which, at Christmas, adorn an otherwise bare fir tree. To see them in this context, rather than in the rarefied, neutral space of the art gallery is the key to understanding whence they spring artistically, for their subject matter is essentially domestic and many pieces were made originally, and were thus given away to friends, as gifts.

It is tempting to read Chorley's work as a curious late manifestation of the kind of functional, decorative embroideries – the samplers, pictures, caskets, firescreens, pincushions, slippers and so forth categorised as 'decorative' or 'applied' art by our major museum collections – which were made by women in the past who for social and economic reasons did not have access to the materials and institutional frameworks associated with the production of 'fine' art. But it would be a mis-reading of work which, while not intellectualised, is far from unlearned and which, however unpretentious the circumstances in which it is produced, is never subsumed by banality or mundanity.

Certainly, Primmy Chorley deeply admires many aspects of traditional 'women's work' – the craft skills applied to and the time invested in functional objects made for the home or for those whom one loves, the use of those objects as a vehicle for storytelling and self-expression, the therapeutic quality of the stitching itself. And in common with the children's drawings and historical embroideries which have been a source of inspiration – the Bayeux Tapestry and the 17th-century raised embroidery known as stumpwork – her work appears simple and unaffected. Her pictures lack illusionistic depth, the figures in them are two-dimensional and highly stylised, their features barely delineated. Almost iconic, they possess an other-worldliness which is a key feature of Chorley's singular vision. Her style was forged during the early 1970s when, as an undergraduate student at Goldsmiths College in South London, she made a study of work produced in art therapy sessions in psychiatric hospitals and was profoundly affected by the art made by some of the residents. Spontaneous, unmuddied by artistic training or received knowledge, it shared with children's art a freedom of expression and an exploration of psyche which she admired and subsequently tried to capture in her own work.

Her attempt was not without its artistic precedents. In the early part of the 20th century Paul Klee, Picasso and others turned for inspiration to art outside the mainstream Western tradition – tribal, folk

left: For you Jessie (detail) – *right:* Mrs Maud

and prehistoric art, for example – as alternatives to what was increasingly being perceived of as rather sterile academicism, and, indeed, an interest in psychotic art was an important impulse in both Expressionism and early Surrealism. Part way through her course Chorley openly turned her back on the kind of training in technique which was *de rigueur* in the Goldsmiths' embroidery department under Constance Howard (who retired as Head of Department in the same year, 1975, that Chorley graduated) and began to work in a more intuitive, uninhibited manner. It is, perhaps, to Goldsmiths' credit that while her work may have perplexed some of her tutors, its intrinsic merits and individuality were still recognised,

Man with two Acrobats

for she was awarded a First Class degree.

There is a sense in which Chorley's art is also produced outside the artistic mainstream, although it knowingly borrows from a roll call of other artistic sources which range from the frescoes of Giotto and Fra Angelico to Coptic textiles, dolls' houses and the work of 20th-century artists such as Stanley Spencer and Gwen John. She has now lived for almost two decades in a fairly isolated community, has educated her two children at home, outside the state education system, and rarely exhibits her work, the production of which was, until very recently, squeezed into the small pockets of time not spent on keeping house, managing a vegetable garden and earning a modest livelihood. What began as a brave attempt at college to throw off tradition and precedent increasingly appears to subvert and, in a sense, challenge the very definitions of what constitutes value in art.

Like folk art with which it has much in common, Chorley's embroidery

has not really developed technically during the past two decades, for technical ambition is not the force which drives it. Since the gauntlet throwing of her time at Goldsmiths she has restricted the number of stitches employed to a very few, mainly stem stitch and buttonhole stitch, the latter being used to secure the appliquéd fabrics which are the distinctive feature of her work. In common with most textile artists she works in cloth for its textures, and recycles any interesting fabrics which are to hand but especially homespun wools and flannels and faded cotton velvets. Recycling is not purely an economic impulse, but an aesthetic one also. She works in a highly intuitive way, without a plan for the finished piece of embroidery, although she does keep sketchbooks of things she wishes to remember. As a student, she remembers making drawings of the historic dolls and dolls' houses at the Museum of Childhood in Bethnal Green; now it might be pieces of used china or interesting domestic detail in old houses, even snatches of poems or phrases read

Love and Happiness

or heard on the radio, anything which holds a resonance for her. But each new piece of work represents, to a large extent, a journey into the unknown.

These intensely personal explorations of her own history and psyche, what she describes as 'stitched memories' can, at times, make the viewer feel like an intruder. Chorley's creations have an enigmatic quality and resist complex interpretation. As stories they yield so much, but no more. Two major series of works have been made during the past decade. The first, a set of panels which she made for the Embroiderers' Guild exhibition *In Context* in 1991, tells the story of her life in West Malling, Kent from 1978–83 – the highs (domestic happiness, for example, in the panel called 'love and happiness' is symbolised by the washing on the line, the 'border' of well-loved kitchenware and the three family dogs, or by the birth of a child in the panel 'and Joseph is born'), the lows ('despair' with its emotions reflected in the dark-coloured

fabrics) and the mixed feelings expressed in 'The Goodbye'. Angels loom large in all of Chorley's work. In 'and Joseph is born' they are larger in size than the human protagonists, while in 'it's alright', probably the most enigmatic of the panels, they swarm protectively around the mother pushing her pram. She reassures her children, is strong for them; the angels look out for all of them. Chorley is not a practising Christian but her work can feel deeply spiritual. The panel 'and Joseph is born' evokes nothing less than a medieval Nativity scene embroidered on some vestment or altar frontal, or rendered in paint by one of the *trecento* or *quattrocento* Italian artists whose work she admires.

In recent years the angels and other figures in Chorley's work have taken on three-dimensional

left: Birth (and Joseph is Born) (detail)

right: The Goodbye

far right: Black Dollies

MR.PINKS
REMOVALS
local & long distance
MOLE END
and
Pikes
all
those
Special
Places
we
loved.
Joey
Jessie
Pinkie
Gyp

form. They appear to have come to life and stepped outside the two-dimensional embroidered pieces. She has since fabricated dozens of these approximately 25 cm high 'dolls' which have a ritualistic, almost totemic quality. Representing ladies and gentlemen, angels and acrobats, they are curiously compelling, slightly disturbing with their mask-like features and lack of hair but, one feels, essentially benign.

Primmy Chorley's most recent work is a set of six tea cosies. While feminist art historians and many textile artists themselves struggle with the terminology of textiles in order to free them of their domestic connotations, what is one to make of an artist like Chorley insisting that she makes objects as functional, mundane even, as tea cosies? Except that these are tea cosies with a difference. If all of her work may be said to be enigmatic, the meaning of these new pieces is positively elusive, and therein lies their power, a power to speak to the deepest human emotions. Because they are

Angels

Tan-yr-Allt II

created outside of contemporary fashions in the visual arts and without a thought for the expectations of art critics, or even another viewer, the spectator must rely on his or her own perceptions and sensibilities in interpreting them. If drawn, Chorley will describe the subject of the 'Paradise Gardens' tea cosies as 'family memories' and affectionate goodbyes to those who were close but are gone – in 'Flowers for Tinker' to one of her much loved dogs, in 'The Garden of Love – for Lin' to her best friend. Chorley's life has clearly been difficult, and tragic at times, but it has also contained much happiness. The naïvety of the slightly whimsical houses and gardens depicted on the tea cosies, and their ubiquitous guardian angels, somehow express this sense of comfort and reassurance – things will be 'alright'. In this way, these deeply personal expressions of joy and grief have a universal resonance.

They are about nothing less than human relationships, life and death.

In common with others who have produced art outside the cultural norm, there is a sense in which Primmy Chorley's art is not at the margins but at the very centre of what artistic creativity can begin to convey.

Jennifer Harris
February 2001

above and right: Teatime in The Garden of Love

above and left: The Cottage in The Garden of Love
and Flowers for Tinker (details)

above and right: Teatime in the the vegetable garden
and Tinker and the Angel (details)

One day the woman saw some most luscious rapunzels. She must eat some or die. Her husband loved her dearly so at night he entered the garden and stole some for her. She made a delicious salad.

left: Mr and Mrs Rapunzel

right: The Dancing Dolls in the Garden (detail)

Curriculum Vitae

Born   1951

Education and work experience

1967–69   Ware College, Herts., – Diploma in Display Design – Winner of Best
          Student Award
1969   Display Artist, Liberty's Department Store, Regent Street, London
1970   Display Artist, Hector Powe, Regent St, London
1971   Assistant to Ken Carr paper sculptor, fabricating large scale paper
          structures for leading London stores (Liberty, Scotch House etc.)
1971–72   St Albans School of Art, Herts., Foundation Course, Art and Design
1972–75   Goldsmith's College, University of London BA Hons (First Class)
          Embroidery Textiles

Awards

1969   Winner of Best Student Award – Ware College, Herts.
1972   Royal Society of Arts Travel Bursary to Turkey, for study of Turkish
          textiles and archaeological artefacts
1987   National Eisteddfod of Wales, Porthmadog – Joint Winner, Embroidery
          Competition

Exhibitions

1987   National Eisteddfod of Wales, Porthmadog – Arts and Crafts Exhibition
1990   Aberystwyth Arts Centre – 'In the First Place'
1990   Oriel 31, Newtown – Group show
1990   Oriel Pendeitsh, Caernarfon – 'Gwynedd Craft'
1991   Hampton Court Palace, London, Embroiderers' Guild – 'In Context'
1992   Crafts Council Gallery, Islington (and extensive tour) – 'Out of the
          Frame'
1992   National Eisteddfod of Wales, Aberystwyth – Arts and Crafts Exhibition
1995   Newbury Arts and Music Festival Arts Workshop – 'Idea and Image'
1995   Fishguard Arts and Music Festival
2000   Alexandra Palace, Knitting and Stitching Show – 'Waves at Goldsmiths'
2001   The Gallery Ruthin Craft Centre, North Wales – Solo Exhibition

List of plates (sizes in mm)

right: Mrs Noah – *far right:* For Dorothy

Published by The Gallery, Ruthin Craft Centre
Text © the authors and RCC 2001
ISBN 1 900941 37 6
Printed by J.T. McLaughlin

Acknowledgements

Ruthin Craft Centre would like to thank and acknowledge the assistance
of the following: Dr Jennifer Harris; the Arts Council of Wales Visual Art
and Craft Department; Christine Mills; Eleri Mills; Audrey Walker; Eirian
and Denys Short; Rozanne Hawksley; Dr Russell; Jill Piercy; Dewi
Tannatt Lloyd; Shawn Stipling; Dave Lewis; Hafina Clwyd; Fennah
Podschies; Simon Sayer; Seàn Harris; Pete Goodridge.

Primmy Chorley would like to thank and acknowledge the assistance of:
all those who have helped and supported her during the development of
this exhibition – 'particular thanks to friends Eirian and Denys Short,
Christine Mills, Eleri Mills, Audrey Walker and Roz Hawksley – and most
of all to my children Joe and Jess for always being there for me'.

Designed by aquarium 01244 398004
Photography by Dewi Tannatt Lloyd

Ruthin Craft Centre Exhibition staff
Philip Hughes & Jane Gerrard

'Primmy Chorley' is a Ruthin Craft Centre Exhibition with support from
the Arts Council of Wales.

This exhibition catalogue is also available in a Welsh Language Version.

The Gallery Ruthin Craft Centre
Park Road, Ruthin, Denbighshire, North Wales LL15 1BB
Tel: 01824 704774

Ruthin Craft Centre is part of Denbighshire County Council.

above: The House of Memories (after I went to 'Cae'r Lloi')
and the House under the Tree (details)

right: Despair (detail)